BRIEF

D0818993

# HOW TO
# WALK INTO
# CHURCH

## TONY PAYNE

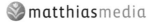

*How to Walk into Church*
© Matthias Media 2015


Matthias Media
(St Matthias Press Ltd ACN 067 558 365)
Email: info@matthiasmedia.com.au
Internet: www.matthiasmedia.com.au
Please visit our website for current postal and telephone contact
information.

Matthias Media (USA)
Email: sales@matthiasmedia.com
Internet: www.matthiasmedia.com
Please visit our website for current postal and telephone contact
information.

ISBN 978 1 922206 72 5

Series design by affiniT Design, typesetting by Lankshear Design.

*Look carefully then how you walk, not as unwise but as wise...* EPHESIANS 5:15

# CONTENTS

# 1. HOW TO WALK INTO CHURCH

I suppose it must have happened upwards of 2000 times by now.

I exit the car, usually with a wife and various kids in tow, and amble in the front door, tossing off a quick greeting to whomever is handing out the folded sheets of paper that in church-speak are called 'bulletins'.[1]

After a quick scan of the seating situation—who has already parked themselves where, who I might want to avoid and so on—I choose a spot not too near the front and sidle into the chosen row, smiling feebly at the person sitting on the other side of the seat that I've politely left vacant between us.

---

1   Or 'handouts'. Or 'newsletters'. Or 'outlines'. Or...

And there it is. I've walked into church.

Not exactly a taxing or impressive feat, and hardly worthy of having a book written about it, even a very short book like this.

But things are rarely as simple as they seem.

It doesn't take very much thought to realize that walking into church is a much more complicated and important subject than it first appears.

In reality there are countless different ways to walk into church.

For example, if it's your first time walking into a particular church then you might be wondering what sort of place it is, whether you'll recognize anyone, and whether it will be possible to avoid that enthusiastic-looking usher making a beeline for you. You might walk in hesitantly or apprehensively, with a murmuring hope in your heart that you'll find answers today to the questions that haunt you. You might be walking into church for the first time in a very long while.

On the other hand, perhaps you've walked into church every Sunday for so many years that any sense of apprehension, expectancy or searching has long since evaporated. Perhaps you walk into church with the same kind of resigned sag to your shoulders that you have when you walk into the office. You don't have high expectations, and they are quite likely to be met—as they were last week and the week before.

Or perhaps your walk into church will be like mine often was during those years when our five children were all under the age of twelve. After a week of long days and short sleeps, followed by the chaos of getting everyone out the door on a Sunday morning, and culminating in a circus of noise and infighting in the car, I didn't really walk into church. It was more of a stagger, followed by semi-collapse into a seat, followed by lengthy periods of zoning out.

Then again, some of us often walk into church in a manner not too different from walking into a stadium, or a shopping centre, or a movie theatre. We walk into church expecting to participate in some larger experience, or to gain some tangible benefit—something that will inspire and uplift us, something that will help us in our lives, and that will repay the investment we are making by being here on Sunday morning instead of sleeping in.

Of course, many Christians also walk into church with a sense of joyful expectancy. Perhaps that is you most Sundays, or at least a decent number of them. You're looking forward to meeting with God, and with your brothers and sisters in Christ. You're looking forward to the warm encouragement you get just from being with them; to the stimulation and challenge of the preaching; to the joy it is to sing together in praise of God and all that he has done.

How do *you* walk into church?

The answer to that not-so-simple question will partly depend on what sort of church you're walking into—whether it is one riven by division and quarrels, for example. It will also be significantly influenced by how things are going in your own life and whether you got a decent night's sleep the night before.

But most importantly, how you walk into church will be determined by *what you think church is, and what you think you're doing there.*

If you think church is a bit like going to the movies, you might walk in expecting to be entertained or inspired.

If you think church is an opportunity for personal devotion and worship, you'll probably walk in not wanting to interact too much with anyone else.

If you think church is something you have to do in order to 'do the right thing' or stay on God's good side, you'll walk in with a determination to do what needs to be done (and then leave as soon as possible).

But if you were to understand what the Bible says about church—about what church is, and why we go there, and what we're supposed to do while we're there—then there is one particular way of walking into church that you would want to master.

This way of walking into church beautifully expresses what church is and what it's meant to be, and why we're all there.

It is this: we should walk into church *praying about where to sit.*

Why is praying about where to sit the best way to walk into church?

The answer to this somewhat unexpected question is simple: because it expresses perfectly what sort of thing 'church' is, and what we're doing there.

**Firstly**, whenever we pray, we express the bedrock truth that is the foundation of church and of everything: God is the gracious sovereign God, and our lives and purposes are in his hands. He is the Lord whom we serve, and his is the power that upholds the universe.

Whenever we pray, we declare our belief in this sovereign loving God. When we pray, we acknowledge our need, and we put our trust in the God who made us and redeemed us, who rules all things, and who has a purpose for each one of us.

This is just as true for church as for any other part of our lives. When we pray about where to sit in church, we're expressing our trust in God for what will happen in church today. We are looking to him and calling upon him as the Lord of the church.

We are also acknowledging that God is in charge of every aspect of church, and that our ideas and preferences and dreams about what church should be like come a distant second. We all have expectations or desires about what we will do at church, and what we will get out of it. But the church is God's, not ours. The church is saved and assembled and ruled by God through the Lord Jesus Christ. He is the one who calls us together, and in whose presence and for whose glory we meet.

If we walk into church praying, we're putting ourselves in the right posture or frame of mind towards God. We are turning our hearts to the one who is the centre of everything, including church.

**Secondly**, when we pray about where to sit, we're also putting ourselves in the right frame of mind towards *each other*. We have started to think about church as being about someone *other than me*.

This can be quite a mind-shift, but it's a vital one. We come to church not only to be loved and blessed by God, but also to love and bless others around us. We come not to spectate or consume, nor even to have our own personal encounter with God. We come to love and to serve. As we'll see (in a few chapters' time), this focus on loving and serving and encouraging those around us is a prominent theme in the Bible's teaching about our role at church.

So when we pray about where to sit, we're trusting that what we do at church really matters; that God has something important for us to do—in particular, someone he wants us to sit next to, talk with, listen to, pray for and encourage.

Praying about where to sit... who would have thought that such a simple act would have so many benefits?

But so far we've only just scratched the surface of what the Bible says about church and our role at church. We need to dig a little deeper.

# 2. WHAT IS THIS THING WE CALL 'CHURCH'?

Y ou've no doubt heard the cliché, "Church is not the building—it's the people". And that's true enough. In the Bible, a church is made up of people, not bricks and mortar. The word that is translated as 'church' in our Bibles simply means a *gathering* or *assembly* of people.

But it's not just any gathering. It is an assembly called together by God himself, for his own purposes. If we want to understand what church really is then we need to understand what these purposes are, and the go-to place in the New Testament to answer that question is in the book of Hebrews, chapters 10-12.

Now Hebrews is not the easiest or shortest letter in the New Testament—although its unnamed author insists that it is just a brief "word of exhortation"

(Heb 13:22). Much of the letter is taken up with a comparison between Jesus and the old covenant, most likely because the Hebrews to whom the letter was written seem to have been tempted to give up on Christ and go back to the more familiar territory of Moses and the law and the temple sacrifices and all the rest.

In chapter 10 the author is getting to the climax of his argument, which is simply this: the new covenant that God has brought about through Jesus Christ is so vastly superior to the old covenant that you'd be nuts to consider going back.

In particular, through Jesus Christ the massive problem at the heart of the old covenant—and in the heart of every person—has been dealt with. The sin and rebellion that separates us from God has been cleansed and atoned for by the single, once-for-all, completely sufficient sacrifice of Jesus Christ.

This makes all the structures and trappings of the old covenant obsolete. Meeting God is no longer a matter of physical temples and physical sacrifices, and high priests going into the Holy of Holies only once a year—now *we can all* come into God's very presence freely and openly and always, because Jesus has gone before us and blazed a trail in his blood. As the author of Hebrews puts it:

> Therefore, brothers, since we have confidence to enter the holy places by the blood of Jesus, by the new and living way that he opened for us through the curtain, that is, through his flesh, and since we have a great priest over the house of God, let us draw near with a true heart in full assurance of faith, with our hearts sprinkled clean from an evil conscience and our bodies washed with pure water. (Heb 10:19-22)

This of course is the starting point for understanding everything about God's purposes for us, but it is also vital for understanding church.

Church is not another instance of the vain human attempt to do something that gains favour with God (although sadly some churches seem to operate as if this is the case). If not even the sacrifices of the God-given old covenant, offered year after year, could really deal with sin, then what hope do we have of coming up with some sort of religious event or set of practices that will satisfy God and earn his blessing? We can't do it, and we don't need to. Jesus has already done it all. We don't need human priests or mediators or activities to get us to God or to usher us into his presence. That has all been done already, by our "great priest" who is over the house of God.

Through him, we have all been granted access to the very throne room of God.

However, God's extraordinary purpose in Christ was not just to save you and me through the once-for-all work of Christ, but also to save and gather *a great congregation of people for himself*. To put it another way, when we stand forgiven before God through the work of Christ, *we don't stand alone*. As we enter God's presence with confidence, we find ourselves in a vast company of forgiven sinners, just like us, who have been cleansed and justified through the blood of Jesus. There's a whole family of us who can now draw near to God with dumbfounded joy on our faces and the name of Jesus on our lips.

The author of Hebrews paints the most extraordinary picture of this gathering of forgiven saints around the throne of God in chapter 12. In fact, in line with his theme of comparing the old covenant with the new, he contrasts this new assembly that God has called together with the classic Old Testament assembly at Mount Sinai:

> For you have not come to what may be touched, a blazing fire and darkness and gloom and a tempest and the sound of a trumpet and a voice whose

words made the hearers beg that no further messages be spoken to them. For they could not endure the order that was given, "If even a beast touches the mountain, it shall be stoned". Indeed, so terrifying was the sight that Moses said, "I tremble with fear". But you have come to Mount Zion and to the city of the living God, the heavenly Jerusalem, and to innumerable angels in festal gathering, and to the assembly of the firstborn who are enrolled in heaven, and to God, the judge of all, and to the spirits of the righteous made perfect, and to Jesus, the mediator of a new covenant, and to the sprinkled blood that speaks a better word than the blood of Abel. (Heb 12:18-24)

In the old covenant, God rescued and redeemed his people out of Egypt, and gathered them around himself at Sinai. But in the infinitely superior new covenant, he has gathered his redeemed people around him in heaven itself, the city of the living God. And just as he did at Mount Sinai, he speaks his word to them—but this time it's the wonderful word of the blood of Jesus.

Do you see yourself in this grand heavenly church? If you're a Christian—someone who has put their trust in Jesus Christ as Lord and Saviour—then you have a place there. You're one of the "assembly [or church] of the firstborn who are enrolled in hea-ven". This is the massive, joyful church that you've "come to", says the author. You're already there in God's presence, because of the "sprinkled blood" of Jesus that allows you to draw near to God with confidence.

Now this assembly is spiritual and heavenly, just as our current relationship with God is. But it is no less real for being so. And there will come a time when this spiritual reality becomes visible for all to see—at the end of time, when the heavenly Jerusalem comes down to earth; when God makes everything new and when Jesus returns to rule in a new creation (see Revelation 21-22 for a stunning description of this).

So this is God's majestic purpose in Christ: to save and redeem and gather around himself a people from every nation, to give them confident access to his own presence, and one day to reveal that mighty assembly of his people in the new creation. In other words, God's purpose in Christ is to build his church.

Now this is all very mind-blowing and encouraging, you might say. But what has it got to do with the very ordinary and decidedly non-heavenly bunch of people that get together every Sunday in that blond brick monstrosity on the corner? What has this heavenly assembly got to do with our earthly assemblies now?

## 2. WHAT IS THIS THING WE CALL 'CHURCH'?

I can answer this question by asking one in return: What has your spiritual, heavenly relationship with God in Christ got to do with your everyday Christian life now? The answer of course is: everything! Precisely because we are *now* God's forgiven, redeemed children through Christ, and *now* have access to his heavenly throne, and *now* have a guaranteed place in his eternal kingdom—on the basis of all these wonderful spiritual realities, God calls us to live a completely different life day by day, not to earn his grace but because his grace has already been showered on us.

In fact, the very reason that God's grace has appeared in Christ and saved us is *so that* we can be liberated to live a new life now day by day, leaving behind the sin and ungodliness of our former lives. As Paul puts it:

> For the grace of God has appeared, bringing salvation for all people, training us to renounce ungodliness and worldly passions, and to live self-controlled, upright, and godly lives in the present age, waiting for our blessed hope, the appearing of the glory of our great God and Saviour Jesus Christ, who gave himself for us to redeem us from all lawlessness and to purify for himself a people for his own possession who are zealous for good works. (Titus 2:11-14)

It's the same with church. The very reason God has saved us is so that we will be part of his eternal church (his assembly, his congregation), and so he calls us now to gather together as his people, as we wait for the time when that great congregation from every nation will be revealed for all to see. Because God has already called us into that heavenly assembly around his throne, we also gather in local assemblies here and now.

So what is it that we're walking into, when we walk into church each week?

We're walking into a gathering that God himself has called together, as part of his majestic plan to save and gather his people around the Lord Jesus Christ. We're walking into an outpost or foretaste of the great spiritual, heavenly assembly of the people of God.

I'm not going to tease out all the implications of this here—and there are many—except to say that because our earthly regular local assemblies are really based on the heavenly assembly that they look forward to, they take on a massive significance and they share a lot of the same characteristics. That is:

- God is present and at the centre of our earthly gatherings, just as he is in the heavenly church (e.g. Matt 18:20; 1 Cor 3:16).
- We get to belong to the local earthly gathering on exactly the same basis as the heavenly one—that is, we belong because Jesus has died to rescue and redeem us from sin; he has purchased our membership with his blood (e.g. Acts 20:28).
- Jesus speaks to us now by his word in our earthly churches, just as he speaks in the heavenly assembly (e.g. Col 3:16; 1 Tim 4:13).
- We respond to Jesus like the multitudes do around the heavenly throne, in joyful trust and thanksgiving and submission to his will.

Of course, there is one important feature of our earthly gatherings that the heavenly church *doesn't* share. It's rather obvious (three letters, starts with 's'), and it is the basis for one of the most important purposes of our earthly gatherings.

That's what we need to consider next: given we now understand more of what church actually is, why do we go there each week?

# 3. WHY AM I WALKING INTO CHURCH?

Given all that we have seen so far, the question "Why go to church?" seems almost crazy. Why *wouldn't* you want to be part of the assembly of God's own people?

But not everyone sees it that way, and if we're honest most of us don't always manage to see it that way. It's common for Christians to wonder (to themselves or out loud) whether there is really very much point in going to church, given how imperfect and mediocre church can often be.

In fact, some people regard the church, with all its imperfections and hypocrisies and institutional failures, as an impediment to the Christian life that we'd be better off without. Can't we just be

Christians, and read our Bibles and pray, and get on with following Jesus? Why all the hassle with church?

Some Christians, even if they don't openly express these sentiments, live as if they believe them—judging by the irregularity of their attendance. They seem to regard church as something of an optional extra, a possibly helpful supplement to their Christian lives, to be utilized only when there is nothing more pressing to go to.

So why do we go to church?

I want to outline two important answers to this question, the first briefly and the second in more detail. **The first answer** flows straight out of what we were looking at in the last chapter. The most basic reason we go to church is simply that *we belong together around God*. It's what we were made for, and what God has saved us for. His whole purpose in Christ is to save and gather his people around himself, and our local churches are the manifestation of that purpose here and now.

To put it another way, we've been adopted into God's eternal family. Questioning why Christians need to gather together in local churches is like asking why families need to get together. It's inconceivable that they wouldn't, and a tragedy when long-held feuds and hurts prevent them from doing so. Families hang out together, talk together, share joys and sorrows, eat together, and generally love each other. It's what families do, because they share such a deep bond with one another.

And likewise with church—except that the bond we share is far more profound. It's a spiritual family bond created by God himself through his Spirit and the Lord Jesus Christ. You could say that our local weekly church meetings are like a long-running weekly family dinner in preparation for the gigantic family reunion that is coming when the Day finally dawns.

That's what we're walking into when we walk into church—a family gathering that God the Father himself has called together, as part of his majestic plan to save and gather his people around the Lord Jesus Christ.

**The second answer** is the one that the author of Hebrews gives. He was worried that his readers were neglecting to meet together. Perhaps his Jewish readers were reasoning that because they no longer needed a physical temple at which to meet God or draw near to him—they now had access to God through Jesus—they didn't need to get together with other Christians at all.

Whatever the background, he urges his readers not to give up on their local church gatherings:

> And let us consider how to stir up one another to love and good works, not neglecting to meet together, as is the habit of some, but encouraging one another, and all the more as you see the Day drawing near. (Heb 10:24-25)

Don't make a habit of staying away, he says, but instead consider how you might stimulate one another to love and to good deeds, and encourage one another to keep going. And they should do so all the more as they "see the Day drawing near".

What is the author's point here? Why should the coming of "the Day" motivate Christians to get together for mutual encouragement and love?

From what the author says consistently throughout the letter, the reason is simple enough: we may be signed-up members now of the heavenly "assembly of the firstborn", and be longing for the Day when it will finally be revealed for all to see—but in the meantime we still suffer the effects of sin, in all its many forms.

Christians live in a world that opposes God and that is often hostile to his people. We live with our own failures and weaknesses, and with the ongoing traitorous presence of sin in our lives. As the author says back in chapter 3:

> Take care, brothers, lest there be in any of you an evil, unbelieving heart, leading you to fall away from the living God. But exhort one another every day, as long as it is called "today," that none of you may be hardened by the deceitfulness of sin. (Heb 3:12-13)

The Christian life is like an endurance race, not a quick sprint (let alone a leisurely stroll). Sin is a constant hindrance (12:1). It slows us down and hampers our stride. It might lead us to start losing our confidence (10:35) or to shrink back from our trust in Christ (10:38).

All this makes constant mutual encouragement and exhortation desperately necessary. As we see the Day approaching, we need help and strength to persevere and be ready for its arrival.

This is why Christians need their regular meetings, like alcoholics need theirs. We need to get together with all our fellow reformed rebels and say, "Hi. My name is Tony, and I'm a forgiven sinner whose confidence is in my Lord and Master, Jesus Christ." And, like alcoholics, we need mentors and coaches alongside us saying, "Keep going. Don't go back to sin—you know it's no good for you. Keep your eyes on the goal."

According to Hebrews, and to the New Testament as a whole, this is a vital aspect of what we do when we gather together in the assembly of forgiven sinners that we call 'church'. We spur one another on. We encourage and help one another. We testify to each other about who Jesus is and what he has done. We speak the word of God to each other because that's where Jesus reveals himself to us, in all that he has said and done. We remind and exhort and teach one another about these wonderful truths, and we correct and admonish and train each other—so that we might not only hold fast to our trust in Christ, but abound in love and good works as we wait and long and pray for his return, and for the revelation of that great heavenly assembly of which we are all members.

And just as we are all members together of God's great assembly, so we are all needed at church. We all have a role to play in encouraging and helping and spurring one another on.

This takes us to the other extended passage in the New Testament that talks about the nature of our church gatherings, and what our role is in them: 1 Corinthians 12-14.

This section of Paul's first letter to the Corinthians is famous for its beautiful description of love in chapter 13, read at so many weddings and found on so many sunset posters. But this great 'love' passage is really about church. The one abiding and ultimate principle that should drive everything about our church gatherings is love—not love in the sense of 'I love ice cream', or 'I love playing golf', but love as a constant attitude that seeks the good of other people rather than myself.

Paul's big point is that if we are to be driven by love, our aim at church should be to build up and encourage *other people*—rather than thinking about how much we're getting out of it or whether we've had a chance to exercise our gifts. Love does not insist on its own way or press its own claims. It is not obsessed with its own enjoyment or convenience. Love doesn't complain or grumble, or stay at home in bed because it couldn't be bothered. Love seeks the good of the other—patiently, kindly, truthfully, joyfully, constantly.

In 1 Corinthians 14, Paul also makes clear that the *way* he wants the Corinthians to build one another in love is through how they speak—not in tongues that others don't understand, but in intelligible words that bring the word of God to each other (especially in what he calls 'prophecy').

The details of what Paul means by 'prophecy', and how exactly it should take place, are open to some debate. But Paul's main point is very clear: he wants the Corinthians to come to church with love in their hearts for one another, and to express that love by sharing the truth of God's word with each other in whatever way they can.

Church is not about me. It's not about the experience I have or what I get out of it. Church is a classic opportunity to love my brothers and sisters who are there, by seeking to build them up in Christ.

Of course, in many churches today it's not really like this. There's a very small number doing the building work—that is, speaking God's word to others, and encouraging others and praying—and a large majority either just gratefully accepting it, or going along for the ride.

It's the ministry of the few.

But what we're talking about, and what we see in the New Testament, is the ministry of the *pew*—a ministry that *we all do*, each Sunday, as we all seek to build one another in love.

Is that how you think of church—as a chance to

encourage, build up, love and spur on your brothers and sisters? Or, like the recipients of Hebrews, have you been neglecting this wonderful duty and opportunity?

Perhaps you do agree that church should be a place where we all pitch in and encourage one another in love–but you aren't really sure exactly what to do or where to start.

That's what we're going to look at in the next couple of chapters.

# 4. BEFORE I WALK INTO CHURCH

So you like the sound of coming to church to love and serve others, and encourage them in Christ. You can see that this is one of God's purposes for our church gatherings, and one of his purposes for us as his people who make up the church.

But where to start?

The place to start is even before that moment when we walk into church praying about where to sit. Learning to be an encourager of others at church starts well before we actually get there.

## 1. Go

It starts with the decision to be there every week.

If you think that church is a necessary but slightly

tedious chore, in which you have very little part to play apart from getting some spiritual sustenance for yourself, then your commitment to being there regularly is likely to be wobbly at best. You'll get there when you can. You'll feel a slight pang of guilt when you don't—but certainly not enough of a pang to prevent you from missing it reasonably often, especially when there is something more pressing or attractive to do.

Judging by the attendance statistics in most churches—including the attendance of faithful, solid, Bible-believing Christians—this must be the mindset of more than half the congregation. Because on any given week, around a third of regular attenders *aren't there.*

Why does this happen?

Well of course there are holidays and sickness, and that accounts for some of the weeks we miss. But it's strange how quickly the absent weeks mount up—a family event, children's sport, a tiring week, bad weather, a weekend away, looking after visiting relatives, a late Saturday night, work deadlines, hitting 'stop' instead of 'snooze' on the alarm, and sometimes just couldn't-be-bothered laziness.

In reality, what really stops many of us from turning up more frequently to church is a failure to grasp just how vital the 'ministry of turning up' really is. One of the most important acts of love and encouragement we can all engage in is the powerful encouragement of just being there—because every time I walk into church, I am wearing a metaphorical t-shirt that says, "God is important to me, and you are important to me". And on the back it says, "And that's why I wouldn't dream of missing this".

Similarly, when we stay away for no good reason one week out of three (or more), we send the opposite message.

None of the important things God has for us to do in church each week can happen if we're not there. We can't love people; we can't talk to them and encourage them; we can't gather with them to listen together to God's word. All of this hangs on the rather simple prerequisite of actually being there.

And so perhaps the most important thing you can do before you walk into church is simply to plan to show up—every week—unless some emergency intervenes. Church needs to move into that category of non-negotiable fixtures around which we plan other things.

But it doesn't stop there. There are at least two other very useful things we can do before we walk into church, to prepare ourselves to be loving servants and encouragers. These activities are not only important and powerful but also quite simple. They are well within the reach of all of us, no matter how inadequate we may feel.

## 2. Pray

There's no reason whatsoever to wait until we walk in the church door to pray about our gatherings. Since God is in charge of church (as he is in charge of everything), he is the one to go to if we want our time at church to be fruitful and encouraging and God-glorifying—not only for ourselves but also for our whole church family. There's so much to pray for:

- We can beg God to bring along all those people who are wavering or uncertain about coming, and to overrule in all the mundane details of the meeting so that everything might work together to build up his people.
- We can ask him to be with us, according to his promise, by speaking to us through the preaching, the Bible reading and the other Bible-shaped words that we speak to each other.
- We can ask him to work powerfully by his Spirit in the hearts of every single person who attends, so that whatever their spiritual state is

as they walk in the door, they might have come to know God better by the time they walk out.

- There may be particular people you want to pray about before you turn up to church—people you are concerned about, or people you've been talking with and trying to encourage. You might pray that God would give you the opportunity and the words to say to help them along in their Christian walk.

There's plenty to pray about before you get anywhere near the front door of church on a Sunday. And these are prayers that God has a habit of answering in the affirmative. When I remember to pray about church (either the night before or just before I go), it's quite incredible—actually, we might say quite unsurprising —how often those prayers are answered; that is, how often rich opportunities for encouragement and growth present themselves in church that week, either for me personally or for those around me as we talk together.

## 3. Think

The third thing we can do before we get to church is to use our brains. This is what the writer to the Hebrews urges his readers to do: "And *let us consider* how to stir up one another to love and good works" (10:24). Encouraging and exhorting and stimulating one another to greater love and maturity in Christ is an exercise of the mind. It takes some thought, and this is something we can very usefully do in advance.

For example, we can read the Bible passage that is set down for our meeting and begin to think about what God is saying in it. This not only greatly increases our own benefit from the sermon, but also makes us much more ready to chat about the main ideas with others. In 1 Corinthians 14, Paul notes that the Corinthians came along to their meetings with words ready to share with one another: "When you come together, each one has a hymn, a lesson, a revelation, a tongue, or an interpretation. Let all things be done for building up" (14:26). As they walked in the door at church, they already had something in their pocket ready to share—some word or song lyric or insight or lesson (even in a foreign tongue) that would be of benefit to the church.

The problem in Corinth, of course, was chaos. Everyone was so keen to share their word that the meeting was descending into an unedifying rabble, and so Paul tells them to get their act together, to wait for each other, to only speak one at a time, and so on. This is because the purpose of all this assorted gospel speech is not my personal expression or satisfaction but the "building up" of those around me.

Most churches today have the opposite of the Corinthian problem—that is, not an unruly profusion of too many people trying to share their words for the sake of the church, but an entire absence of anyone (except the preacher) having something edifying to share for the building up of God's people.

A very simple way to address this is for all of us to read the Bible passage in advance, reflecting on what God is saying there and bringing those insights with us—ready to use them in an orderly and useful way, if God gives us opportunity.

Of course, if your church doesn't base its sermon on a particular Bible passage, or doesn't tell you what the passage is in advance—well that's unfortunate, and something you might discuss with your pastor. But even then, there is nothing to stop you coming to church with some words in your pocket to share, perhaps from your own Bible reading during the week.

If we understand what church really is, and what our role is in the gathering, then we'll be well-prepared as we walk in the door—prayerfully expectant that God is going to work powerfully in our gathering, and ready to do our part in his work.

# 5. AFTER I WALK INTO CHURCH

So you've made it in the front door, having prayed and thought in advance, and with a silent prayer on your lips about where to sit. What then? What can you do during the church meeting itself to love and encourage and serve other people?

You might be thinking, "Well, not much really". After all, most of the interactions that normally happen in church take place between us and God—that is, we hear God speak to us through his word (as it is read and taught); we respond to him in thanksgiving and prayer and in song; we remember his death on the cross for us and put our trust in him; we confess our sins to him and rejoice in his forgiveness.

All this feels more 'vertical' than 'horizontal', as

people often describe it. Surely our focus in church should be on God, and not so much on each other.

This is only half true. Of course our church meetings are all about God and should focus on him and the Lord Jesus Christ. In fact, as we've already seen, we only gather in church because of what God has already done in gathering us to himself in Christ. He has 'come down' to us, and become one of us, and reconciled us to himself through Jesus, our one and only mediator and advocate. And our church meetings also have this character. God takes the initiative in church; he 'comes down' to meet with us through his word and Spirit, and we respond to him in repentance and faith.

So of course church is very 'vertical'; it's all about relating to God through the Lord Jesus Christ. But the more we focus on Jesus, the more clearly we see through his eyes the people sitting all around us, for whom he died. The better we come to know the God who sacrificed his Son for the salvation of all of us, the more our hearts are filled with love for the motley crew of forgiven sinners who are our brothers and sisters in Christ.

Church is not a kind of trade-off between the 'vertical' and the 'horizontal'—between the 'vertical' actions of encountering God and the 'horizontal' activities of talking with and encouraging each other. You cannot separate these two. In fact, it is often very hard to figure out which parts of our church life are 'vertical' and which 'horizontal'. When someone reads the Bible, something very 'vertical' is happening—the very word of God is being spoken in the congregation. And yet it is also a very 'horizontal' action, because God's word has only been heard on account of the fact that Mrs Thurgood has limped up to the microphone, announced the reading, waited for what seems like ten minutes for everyone to find the place, and then falteringly read the words in a manner that makes plain that this is the first time she has ever clapped eyes on them.

What we do in church is a constant interplay between encountering God and encountering the people around us.

So, practically speaking, how do we love and serve and encourage our brothers and sisters during our church gatherings? What does this look like?

It's likely to look different for each one of us, and from Sunday to Sunday, because our churches are all different and we each have different opportunities and possibilities from one week to the next to love God and the people around us. But here are three examples to get you started.

## 1. When we sing

When we sing, our hearts are often stirred and lifted up to God. As Paul puts it, we make melody to the Lord in our hearts (Eph 5:19). We can thank him in song, and pray to him in song, and express in so many different ways our delight and joy and amazement and gratitude and love to our heavenly Father and the Lord Jesus Christ.

But when we sing, we also teach and exhort one another, and declare to one another the great deeds and words of the Lord. Singing is an act of edification and mutual encouragement as much as an act of God-ward thanksgiving and joy. In fact, when we look at what 'praise' is in the Bible, especially in the psalms, we find that it almost always has this dual focus or audience. It is directed to God in thankfulness and joy for all that he is and has done. But it is also directed to those who are listening, that they too might recognize the greatness of God and rejoice and give thanks to him. Praise is like advertising—it begs for an audience.

This means that no matter what the song, it's always more encouraging and helpful if you sing it with gusto—as opposed to mumbling out the words with a bored or peevish look on your face, which encourages no-one. It does not matter whether you like this particular song, or whether the musicians are any good, or even whether you are any good at singing—you belt out the song with enthusiasm, because as you do you're really giving voice to your faith in God and hope in God and love for God. But you're also testifying to those around you. You're being an example and an encouragement to the rest of the congregation.

## 2. When we listen

You might think the sermon is one occasion when we are definitely just focusing on God and not others; we are just in listening and receiving mode, not contributing and helping mode. But there is actually a lot we can do to help both the preacher and our fellow congregation members during the sermon. It makes an enormous difference to the preacher if the congregation is listening actively and with engaged attention, and if we show this by nodding, making eye contact, taking notes, and laughing at the jokes (even the old ones). This spurs on the preacher in his ministry and gives him heart.

Our active listening also infects others around us— just as our bored, disengaged listening discourages them. So think for a moment: what does your facial 'screen saver' during sermons say to the preacher and to those around you? What do they see when they look at you listening to the sermon?

My mate Ben Pfahlert says he commonly sees four screen savers on the faces of people he preaches to.

There's the Shar Pei Dog, who presents a permanently grumpy, closed-off expression that makes clear to everyone that nothing and nobody is going to get through to him.[2]

There's the Invisible Fairy Hunter, whose eyes flit everywhere, counting the bricks and checking out the ceiling, like Captain Hook in search of Tinker Bell.

Then there's the Stunned Mullet, who has on his face the expression of someone who has just been administered horse tranquilizer.

And of course we have all seen (or been) the Dipping Duck, who is struggling mightily to remain awake, and whose head drops slowly into unconsciousness only to startle awake and begin the process all over again.

Have a think about your facial 'screen saver', and whether the way you listen is an encouragement or discouragement to others.

---

2  If you don't know what a Shar Pei dog looks like, we've included a photo of one at the end of the book.

## 3. The nuts and bolts

Loving the people around you at church can also be expressed in the little things—like the thoughtfulness that notices the person next to you doesn't have a Bible, and offers to share. It's expressed in a servant-hearted attitude that does whatever it can to help others around them.

For example, what do you normally do if you notice that it's a bit hot and stuffy in church? My tendency is to get a bit grumpy and then complain afterwards to someone in authority. But the loving, servant-hearted thing would be to quietly slip out of my seat and open a window, or find someone who can check that the ventilation has been turned on. Love sees a need and tries to meet it, rather than seeing a problem and doing nothing about it—or, worse, complaining about it.

Another obvious example of loving thoughtfulness is in our care for newcomers. If we see someone who looks new, we should look after them. They're a guest at our family gathering. It's not the pastor's gathering; it's God's and ours. And just as God has so generously welcomed us, so we should welcome our guests. We should sit next to them, perhaps as a result of praying about where to sit. And we should be attentive to them, helping them find their way during the service. They might need help in following along, or they might need to be introduced to the crèche or the children's programs. We should treat newcomers like the honoured guests that they are.

And we should be especially looking out for newcomers and caring for them in that 'after church' time that is not really after church.

# 6. WHEN CHURCH FINISHES BUT DOESN'T

For some people, the last song or the closing benediction at church is like the starter's gun—it's their cue to make a rapid exit to the car park.

This hardly seems to reflect an attitude of loving service and sacrifice. But it raises an interesting question: *When does church actually finish?*

So far we've seen that church is not just the series of activities we do together—the preaching, the songs, the collection, the announcements. Church is *us*—the joyful gathering of God's people in his presence, where we build each other in love through his word.

But if that's the case, then church doesn't really finish when it finishes—that is, when we conclude the formal activities that we normally do together. If we continue to meet together informally over tea and coffee, then... we're still gathering. It is 'after church', but in another sense it's not really after church at all. And it's often during this informal church time that we are presented with prime opportunities to encourage and love and build up other people.

How can we do this?

The basic method follows on from all that we've seen so far in this book. If we want to encourage and build people in our conversations at church, the key thing is to speak God's word. We grow in Christ, and gain encouragement and strength and hope, when we understand the truth and put our trust in it. And the source of that truth about God and Christ and the world and one another is in the words that God himself speaks to us in the Bible.

This is why our church gatherings are centred on hearing God's word and responding to what we hear. If we want to encourage each other in conversation, then the word of God should be the theme and the topic of what we talk about.

The Scriptures themselves urge us to do this. In 1 Thessalonians 4, after talking about the great Christian hope of the return of Jesus and the eternal life we will share with him, Paul says to his readers: "encourage one another with these words" (v. 18). Likewise, in Colossians 3:16, he says: "Let the word of Christ dwell in you richly, teaching and admonishing one another in all wisdom".

As we talk with each other in our congregation, this is the essential way in which we build and encourage one another in love: by speaking the word to each other.

"But", you might be thinking, "I don't feel very knowledgeable, and I'm not very good at starting these sorts of conversations. I usually end up just chatting about the kids, or how things are at work, or the football, or making other small talk. How can I actually encourage someone in conversation?"

As always, the first thing is to pray—pray before church that God would use you to bring encouragement to people today, and pray during the church meeting that God would open up opportunities for you to have encouraging conversations. God has a habit of answering prayers like that.

The easiest way to get such a conversation started is to bounce off the sermon that you've all just heard. Over coffee, you might ask your friend, "What did you get out of the sermon today?", and that might get something going. But often a really general question like that leaves people stumped. It's usually better to say something more specific. As you're listening to the sermon, jot down a question that you have or a key point that really challenged you, and then share that with someone after church. You might say, "That was really interesting what the pastor said this morning about forgiveness. I'd never really understood the connection between God forgiving us and us forgiving others. What did you think?"

This will often lead to an interesting and mutually helpful chat over the Word. But even if it doesn't, you've been an encouragement to your friend. You've shown them your enthusiasm for the word, and for listening to the sermon. That sort of thing is an infectious example to set.

The word of God is the best foundation for an encouraging conversation, but you can build on this foundation in all sorts of ways.

For example, you can talk with others about how they (and you) came to salvation in Christ. Sometimes we're in church with people for years without knowing how they became a Christian. Why not start a conversation on Sunday like this: "Phil, I don't know if I've ever heard how you became a Christian. How did it happen with you?" This almost always leads to a warm and encouraging conversation, where you can both reflect on the wonder of God's grace to us in Christ.

Another simple way to get an encouraging conversation started is to ask the person if there is anything they'd like you to pray for them. In my experience, this simple question almost immediately takes your conversation to a different level. It prompts people to think about how God relates to their daily lives and what they would like to bring before him. And it expresses your care for them and your desire to help (by praying). You can even finish off by praying, right then and there. It should be quite normal and ordinary for Christians to pause in their conversations and pray for one another. Just say, "OK, I might just pray briefly about that now". And lead in a short prayer.

Another obvious way to love and serve over coffee is to be on the lookout for newcomers, who often find this informal time a bit awkward. Take care of them, introduce them around, find out their background and their story, give them some information about the church, invite them back to your place for lunch (or dinner). In other words, keep being a good host. This is a huge encouragement for new people.

There are lots of ways we can build other people up in love in our informal conversations over coffee. There is no shortage of opportunities—in fact, if our eyes are opened to see it, there are people all around us who want and need encouragement and help to know Christ and to live for him, because they are struggling, fallible people just like us.

If we begin to grasp this, we won't see the informal coffee time as an awkward social time to escape from, nor as a chance simply to catch up on the latest with our friends. We will see it for what it is: a place where God is still present in the midst of us, leading us to love and encourage one another through his word.

# 7. HOW TO WALK OUT OF CHURCH

In this little book, we have by no means been able to say everything about what church is or what we should do there. But we have seen that church exists because of the work of God through the Lord Jesus Christ. He calls and saves us into a great assembly of the people of God, gathered in Christ around his heavenly throne—an assembly we're already enrolled in now, and already belong to now, but which won't be revealed here on earth until Christ returns in his glory.

In the meantime, in the midst of the sin and evil of this world, God calls his saved people together into the local assemblies that we call 'churches'. In these we gather together in his presence to hear his word, to respond joyfully to him in thanksgiving and prayer, and to love and encourage one another as we wait for the Day when Jesus returns.

All of which means that we come to church each week as grateful, loving, other-person-oriented members of God's people, ready not only to encounter God and respond to him, but to encounter our brothers and sisters and love them as well.

Over the last few brief pages, we've looked at how this biblical wisdom would affect our 'walk' at church—what we do before we come to church, and what we do when we get there (both in the formal part of the meeting and during the informal time afterwards).

The Bible often uses 'walking' as a way of talking about the course of our everyday lives. For example, the apostle Paul tells the Ephesians to "Look carefully then how you walk, not as unwise but as wise, making the best use of the time, because the days are evil" (Eph 5:15-16).

Our 'walk' is our daily progress through the world; our 'journey' as it is often called these days. In our walk, we can be wise or unwise. We can make our way through life with an understanding of the days we live in and what they require, or we can meander along in an ignorant daze.

So it is with our 'walk' at church—that is, as we

walk in and walk around and walk out again. We can make our way through church with a true and wise understanding of just what church is, what is really happening there, and what the situation demands of us. Or we can stumble along not really knowing why we are there or what we are doing.

What about the final part of that walk– the walk out of church?

The first and most painful thing we need to face is that many people walked out of church a long time ago and have not come back. People leave church for different reasons, but it often comes down to one of two basic attitudes:

- *Church is not satisfying to me.* I am just not getting enough out of it–whether inspiration, community, relationships, answers, joy, fulfilment, spiritual nourishment, a stronger relationship with God, or whatever it is I'm looking for. It's just not really worth my time any more.
- *Church has seriously burned me.* I've experienced a personal conflict, abusive or manipulative leadership, disillusionment due to the hypocrisy of a trusted friend or leader, or something similar. I'm just done with it.

Within these two categories, there may well be good reasons for walking away from a particular church. It may be that a particular church has strayed so far from the gospel and the Bible that it is no longer a place where you can gather around the word of God with other believers—because the word of God isn't really there any more. Or it may be the case that the unrepentant bad behaviour of leaders or members in a particular congregation makes it untenable for you to continue there. Leaving a church is a very serious thing to do, but sometimes it is necessary.

But what we're talking about here is not the painful, last-resort decision to leave one church and join another, but the temptation that nearly all of us have experienced at one time or another to drift away from the church we're going to and never make it into another one.

If what we have seen from the Scriptures about church is true, this really isn't an option for Christian believers. God calls us into the family of his people. And even though that family is often hard to live with, and is full of sinful people just like us... well, they're still family, and we still have the obligation and privilege to love and serve them (and we still need them to do the same for us). That's something that can't happen if we give up going to the regular family gathering called 'church'. It's not just that we ourselves need the encouragement and help of our fellow believers to keep persevering in the Christian life; it's also that *they need us*.

You might be reading this as someone who is sorely tempted to walk out of church and not come back. Maybe you already have. Or perhaps you still turn up most weeks, out of a sense of duty or so as not to make waves in your family, but you departed mentally and emotionally some time ago. You're there but you're not really there.

If that's you, then look again at the words that God spoke through the apostle Paul all those centuries ago: "Look carefully then how you walk, not as unwise but as wise, making the best use of the time, because the days are evil" (Eph 5:15-16). The walk that takes you out of church and away from church—whether figuratively or literally—is not a clever one. It ends up causing you to waste your time on things that don't really matter and don't really last. It doesn't recognize that the times we live in are evil. And, most seriously, it's a walk away from God's purposes for you, both now and in eternity.

So much for the foolish way to walk out of church. What would be the wise way?

The wise way would be to walk out of church with the word of God on our lips and in our hearts, ready to submit every part of our lives to the Lord Jesus Christ. I love the way Paul puts this in his letter to the Colossians:

> Put on then, as God's chosen ones, holy and beloved, compassionate hearts, kindness, humility, meekness, and patience, bearing with one another and, if one has a complaint against another, forgiving each other; as the Lord has forgiven you, so you also must forgive. And above all these put on love, which binds everything together in perfect harmony. And let the peace of Christ rule in your hearts, to which indeed you were called in one body. And be thankful. Let the word of Christ dwell in you richly, teaching and admonishing one another in all wisdom, singing psalms and hymns and spiritual songs, with thankfulness in your hearts to God. And whatever you do, in word or deed, do everything in the name of the Lord Jesus, giving thanks to God the Father through him. (Col 3:12-17)

Paul captures many of the themes that we've been exploring in this book. It's all there:

- the way God has chosen and called us for himself to be his own holy, forgiven people

- the love that should unite and crown all our behaviour towards each other
- the word of Christ that dwells richly among us as we encourage and admonish each other
- the glad and thankful songs that express our joy at all that God has done.

It's a wonderful description of the Christian congregation in action, and the endpoint is a life where we strive to do everything—every word and deed—in the name of the Lord Jesus.

In the verses immediately following, Paul gives examples of that holy, loving, Jesus-honouring life in action, whether as wives and husbands (Col 3:18-19), as children and parents (3:20-21), as slaves and masters (3:22-4:1), or in our interactions with the non-Christian world day by day (4:5-6).

In other words, we should walk out of our local churches encouraged and stirred up to love and good works (as Hebrews 10 puts it), ready to live for Christ and speak for Christ in every facet and sphere of our lives:

- in our ongoing relationships with our church family, as we continue to care for each other, pray for each other, and meet in smaller groups or one-to-one

- in our marriages and families
- in our workplaces
- in the wider world of relationships in our neighbourhood and community and society.

This is how God wants us to walk, for "we are his workmanship, created in Christ Jesus for good works, which God prepared beforehand, that we should walk in them" (Eph 2:10).

 **matthias**media

Matthias Media is an evangelical publishing ministry that seeks to persuade all Christians of the truth of God's purposes in Jesus Christ as revealed in the Bible, and equip them with high-quality resources, so that by the work of the Holy Spirit they will:

- abandon their lives to the honour and service of Christ in daily holiness and decision-making
- pray constantly in Christ's name for the fruitfulness and growth of his gospel
- speak the Bible's life-changing word whenever and however they can—in the home, in the world and in the fellowship of his people.

Our resources range from Bible studies and books through to training courses, audio sermons and children's Sunday School material. To find out more, and to access samples and free downloads, visit our website:

# www.matthiasmedia.com

## How to buy our resources

**1.** Direct from us over the internet:
– in the US: www.matthiasmedia.com
– in Australia: www.matthiasmedia.com.au

**2.** Direct from us by phone: please visit our website for current phone contact information.

> Register at our website for our **free** regular email update to receive information about the latest new resources, **exclusive special offers**, and free articles to help you grow in your Christian life and ministry.

**3.** Through a range of outlets in various parts of the world. Visit **www.matthiasmedia.com/contact** for details about recommended retailers in your part of the world, including www.thegoodbook.co.uk in the United Kingdom.

**4.** Trade enquiries can be addressed to:
– in the US and Canada: sales@matthiasmedia.com
– in Australia and the rest of the world: sales@matthiasmedia.com.au

**5.** Visit **GoThereFor.com** for subscription-based access to a great-value range of digital resources.

# Fearing God... so we don't have to be afraid

## David Mears

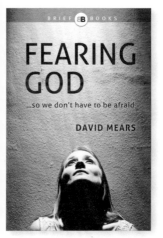

Do you sometimes find yourself feeling embarrassed or uneasy when the idea of 'fearing God' comes up in the Bible? Would you invite your friends and family to a special guest service at church if you knew that was going to be the message?

Fear is taboo in Western society. Fear curtails freedom; it crushes dreams; it inhibits people. It should be avoided altogether.

But some kinds of fear are healthy— just as some kinds of fearlessness are foolish.

There is bad fear and good fear. And, oddly enough, fearing something can mean we are no longer afraid of it.

In this short book, David Mears takes us back to the Bible to look again at the fear of God—and more than that, to take delight in it and discover why the fear of the Lord really is "the beginning of wisdom".

## More Brief Books

# The Everlasting Purpose
## Broughton Knox

In just under 50 pages, former Principal of Moore Theological College Broughton Knox provides an extraordinarily clear and encouraging explanation of the Bible's teaching on predestination. He shows the comfort, assurance and blessing that flow from understanding the nature of God, the nature of man, and the means of our salvation in Christ.

Broughton Knox's clear thinking and steadfast commitment to the Scriptures will help you make sense of a topic that just about every Christian struggles to understand—let alone explain to others.

*First published as 'God who is rich in mercy', a chapter in Broughton Knox's book* The Everlasting God.

FOR MORE INFORMATION OR TO ORDER CONTACT:

**Matthias Media**
Email: sales@matthiasmedia.com.au
www.matthiasmedia.com.au

**Matthias Media (USA)**
Email: sales@matthiasmedia.com
www.matthiasmedia.com